MW00908037

THE
ROAD TO
GREATNESS

HOW TO GET TO WHERE
YOU REALLY WANT TO BE

Moshe Goldberger

TARGUM/FELDHEIM

First published 1997
Copyright © 1997 by Moshe Goldberger
ISBN 1-56871-112-3

Published by:
Targum Press, Inc.
22700 W. Eleven Mile Rd.
Southfield, MI 48034

Distributed by:
Feldheim Publishers
200 Airport Executive Park
Nanuet, NY 10954

Distributed in Israel by:
Targum Press Ltd.
POB 43170
Jerusalem 91430

Printed in Israel

Rebbe Akiva's determination, prayers, and laughter brought hope to our people in their time of need.

This *sefer* is dedicated to

Reb Hirsch Berel
ben
Avraham Leib ע״ה

whose smile and laughter encouraged many to believe that everything will work out for the best.

*Moshe and Shifra Finer
and their children
Ashra, Avi, Hirshi, and Yitzi*

This book has been
prepared with the help of:

Rabbi Eliezer Gevirtz
Rabbi Menachem Goldman
Moshe Finer
Mordechai Gelber
Yehoshua Danese
B. Siegel
Yitzhok Gold
S. Teitler
Danny Lemberg
and others ...

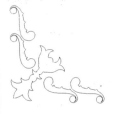

Contents

THREE: Learning to Laugh
with Rabbi Akiva

ONE

Determination

Choices

Are you interested in finding a better job? A *shidduch*? A house? Ways to make more money? To finish *Shas*? To achieve a happier marriage? To pray with more concentration? To learn new skills? To be healthier? To give more *tzedakah*?

The secret lies in applying the teachings of our Sages:

On the path one is determined to go he is led.

(*Makkos* 10b)

One who comes to purify himself will be assisted.

(*Yoma* 38b)

A simple but powerful secret. As the Alei Shur explains in his chapter on *ratzon*, "desire" (vol. 1, p. 120):

> *We have already explained what you should desire and how to achieve these goals, but what is the key? The answer is this secret: the power of determination!*

One needn't be a genius to succeed, or lucky. There is a phrase that summarizes this concept: nothing stands in the way of one who is determined.

You may be poor, uneducated, old, or young — this principle can be applied at any time. Make the choice to be determined, and you will be on the road to greatness.

The Difference

Determination makes all the difference between a person who is successful and one who is not.

What do you want to accomplish with your life? What do you want to become? Do you have a secret ambition?

What great goal would you tackle if you knew you would not fail? What would you do if you received a million dollars now? What would you do if you discovered that you had only six months left to live?

One hint to finding the right answers is the *mishnah* (*Avos* 1:10) that teaches the obligation to love work. Ask yourself: Do you enjoy your daily work activities? Are you successful at what you do? Could you teach others to succeed in what you do for a living? Could you put together a guide entitled, *How to Succeed in Your Profession?*

If you are determined, you can accomplish all these things. But consider: Are you willing to take some risks? Are you willing to give up something in order to get something else?

A writer who won a Pulitzer prize writes that his book became a success from the day he decided that he was determined to go anywhere, talk to anyone, read anything, and try anything that might help him learn more about his book's subject matter. His decision turned up all kinds of extraordinary information. Without his determination he'd be just another writer. Determination makes all the difference.

An Application

How long does it take to become a success? It depends. If you are 100 percent determined to become wealthy, for example, you can do it in about three weeks' time.

1) You would begin by studying in depth the *mishnah* (*Avos* 4:1) that defines true wealth — being happy with what you have. That should take at least a week.

2) Then you would have to apply the lessons of that *mishnah*, which should take about two more weeks. When you learn to appreciate that there is nothing out there that will make you happy, that you become happy solely by learning how to rejoice with your portion in life, you can achieve this great goal.

To apply the *mishnah* you will:

1) Decide firmly to accept the Torah's approach: that you are determined to become rich by learning to appreciate your portion.

2) Repeat and review your decision at least once daily, with enthusiasm and conviction.

3) Visualize yourself as having achieved your new goal. Imagine that you are already happy. Try to feel it now.

4) Act the part.

5) Teach others this new concept you have discovered.

Responsibility

In Rav Avigdor Miller's book *Rejoice, O Youth* (p. 1), he writes:

> *If you wish hard enough, it will happen... Hashem guides a person who seeks wisdom; the measure of guidance is in proportion to the earnestness of the seeker.*

How much are you willing to work at accomplishing your goals? For how long?

Are you sincere in your quest? Hillel would say:

> *If I am not for myself, who will be for me?*
>
> *(Avos* 1:14)

But what about Hashem? Doesn't He do everything? Our Sages teach: "Everything is in the Hands of Heaven..." Hillel surely taught that as well. But which comes first?

On the path one desires to go he is led.

You are the source of the conditions and situations in your life. The way your world looks right now is a result of your decisions and choices. Once you make the choice, Hashem helps you accomplish your goal.

The Maharsha (*Niddah* 59b) questions this concept: Our Sages teach that Hashem determines the level of our wisdom, wealth, etc., before our birth. How, then, can the Gemara teach that we are able to change things?

We never know whether we have achieved the level that was predetermined for us by Hashem. Thus we have to keep trying to do our best to achieve our potential level. In addition, our efforts and prayers can even change the level that was originally set for us. Thus, it is up to each person to develop himself.

Hillel was very, very poor. He could have excused himself by saying, "I can't help it if I was born poor." There were great Sages who were blind, but they did not say, "I am handicapped. It is not my fault." Yosef may have suffered as a slave, and then as a prisoner, but he kept on striving until he became a great ruler. You may think, *How can I change certain things?* But the truth is that it's up to you to make the correct choices!

The tendency, however, is to blame our problems on Hashem. "This must be *bashert*." Translation: Hashem has decided things should be just as they are now. Thus it is not my fault.

Mishlei (19:3) categorizes this view:

The foolishness of man corrupts his path, but he blames it on Hashem.

The truth is that when we learn to comprehend the fact that Hashem is anxiously awaiting our decision in order to help us achieve, we realize we are responsible. We never have an excuse to plead helplessness, because Hashem is on our side, and He is the Ultimate Power.

By thinking, *This situation is my fault, and I can change my situation,* and, *It is up to me to react to this situation in a positive manner,* you can take the actions necessary to reach your potential, which include prayer to Hashem, and then Hashem will help you follow through.

On the Road

The Alei Shur explains that when we speak about *ratzon* , we are not referring to frequent whims, most of which are merely fantasies. Desire refers to a sincere, powerful commitment.

This includes:

1) *A clear idea of your objective.* This means a detailed mental picture of your desire and goals, in a sharp, clear, and specific way. Wanting money is not

specific enough. How much? When? Why? Wanting to change and improve yourself is insufficient. How? When?

If you are as of yet unsure of your objectives, at least determine to discover exactly what you desire in a specific area by a certain time. When our Sages teach this principle, they use the expression "the road on which one desires to go." This teaches us that your goal must be as clear to you as the road you use to reach the bank or shul.

2) *A commitment to focus all your energy on a specific desire that fills your entire essence.* Will you pursue your goal no matter what? Is your goal that important to you? How much is it worth to you? Are you living for it?

Which Path?

What should some of our essential goals be? Some things you might want to accomplish are: to control your anger, arrogance, and selfishness; to be more honest and self-disciplined.

But the underlying core of everything we do is controlled by choosing between one all-inclusive positive character trait and one negative one. The negative trait is to let things happen as they may, without any specific effort on your part to take control. The positive trait is the absolute decision to choose to be in control of your life and to do what is right at all times. This commitment encompasses everything. But it will not succeed if you are only halfhearted in your decision (Chazon Ish, *Emunah U'Bitachon* 4:1). One who complains about his failures, saying, "It's because I need more help from Hashem," is guilty of slandering Hashem, Who has provided us with a guarantee: "Those who come to purify will be assisted." Thus, one's failure is proof that his own efforts were inadequate (*Alei Shur*).

Hashem has provided you with a phenomenal intellect and the power to choose to harness your determination in order to improve your lot in all areas, as we explained above. And it is a fact in life that a person usually achieves that which he truly desires. Obviously, then, the reverse is also true: What a person achieves is a revelation as to what his actual desires are (ibid.).

The Mishnah (*Avos* 2:8) teaches that the great Sage Rabban Yochanan ben Zakkai instructed his five greatest disciples to "go out and see: what is the good way to which a person should cling?" He was not satisfied with the obvious answer — to study Torah and perform all the mitzvos. That was not specific enough. The quest was to focus and ascertain the specific path that ensures one will achieve every form of perfection.

Writing down your goals will assist you in clarifying them. The following are some basic goals that should be found on the top of our lists:

1) To dedicate oneself to working on clear, specific goals every day.

2) To commit oneself to be willing to learn from others how to become better at serving Hashem (*Avos* 4:1).

3) To develop the self-discipline to master and control oneself is one of the most important qualities one must develop (ibid.). This includes developing one's honesty and integrity, coupled with a genuine desire to serve Hashem.

4) To be action-oriented and get on with what needs to be done as soon as possible (now!) and to do it quickly (*Avos* 1:4); to develop and maintain a sense of urgency; to overcome procrastination, push aside fears, and concentrate single-mindedly on using one's time most effectively. One of the best sources for developing these habits is an ongoing review program of *Mesilas Yesharim*'s section on *zerizus*.

5) To focus on getting along with others. It takes a firm decision on our part to cultivate patience, kindness, compassion, understanding, and modesty. (This is also summed up in *Avos* 4:1.)

6) To take care of one's health; to watch one's diet by eating the right foods in the right proportions; to exercise in order to keep fit. Maintaining one's health is one of the most important mitzvos of the Torah for obvious reasons. It is the first step necessary in order to be active in the service of Hashem.

This goal should arguably be the first on this list. However, we have placed it later on because without the right intentions and focus on one's mission in life, this item can easily be corrupted.

To summarize, whatever path you take must be rooted in the positive. Then you must focus on your specific goals.

The Goal

Would you believe me if I suggested that there is nothing in the world that you cannot achieve in five years' time if you were willing to pay the price for it?

Of course, you would ask me for a source. How about the *gemara* in *Megillah* 6b? Let's say you have set for yourself the goal to become a *talmid chacham* (Torah scholar) within the next five years.

> *If you toil in Torah study, you will achieve.*

> (Ibid.)

No exceptions. It may take you five years, but you will succeed if you work hard enough.

(If your goal is to succeed in business, see the source in *Megillah* [ibid.] and the *Maharsha* we mentioned above.)

The big question at this point is deciding which goals are most important for you now. To think you can have *everything* you want may be true, but it will not get you anywhere. You have to focus on specifics.

Running to and From

> *Run to every mitzvah [even an easy one] and flee from sin, because one mitzvah leads to another and one sin leads to another...*

> (*Avos* 4:2)

The Talmudic lesson we began with (see p. 11) uses the word *"rotzeh"* (in the way one desires to go), which is the same root as the one used here for "running" to do mitzvos.

Why is it essential to run to do mitzvos? One explanation, by the Ruach Chaim, is that the running is a mitzvah in itself, for which one will merit to perform the actual mitzvah. Similarly, by performing the mitzvah to flee from sin, one will merit to be saved from the sin.

This explains the mechanism behind the concept of the principle that in the way you are determined to go Hashem will lead you. Your positive decision is a mitzvah in itself, which is then rewarded by Hashem with more success.

To understand this even better we have to realize that the existence of mankind's free will (*bechirah*) is a special miracle by the Creator of the universe. Free will is the greatest miracle after the Creation of the universe (*Rejoice, O Youth*, p. 281). Hashem has created a space in which He allows man to exercise his own free will. The thoughts and decisions of a person are thus more important than the greatest upheavals of nature (ibid., p. 282).

This, Rav Miller (ibid., p. 302) explains, is the reason why one who reviews a Torah lesson 101 times is called a "servant of Hashem," in contrast to one who reviewed the lesson only 100 times (*Chaggigah* 9b). The primary purpose of life is to test a person's free will in the pursuit of perfection. By forcing his mind further ahead, in the struggle toward greater achievement in knowledge of Torah, development of mind and character, and excellence in the love and practice of kindliness and other mitzvos, one is achieving true perfection.

Rabbeinu Yonah (*Sha'arei Teshuvah* 3:17) teaches:

Supreme virtues are available to us by the positive mitzvos which the mind can fulfill, such as...the mitzvah of bechirah [to choose with one's free will], the mitzvah to study Torah...meditating in the greatness of Hashem, thinking about His kindnesses to us...

Rabbeinu Yonah concludes this section with the following declaration:

What hope is there for a created being if he does not invest the toil of soul and his primary efforts in those matters for which he was created?

Our great wish in life should be, "Uncover my eyes so that I may see the wonders of Your Torah" (Tehillim 119:18). The more we repeat this verse and focus on it sincerely, the more Hashem will assist us in making it happen.

Mind Power

The way one looks at the world is the kind of world he shall have (*Sing, You Righteous*, p. 17). This principle, Rav Miller explains, is derived from Mishlei (4:23):

> *Guard your mind more than everything else, for from it come all the results of life!*

Have you ever thought about food and found yourself hungry? Think about a tragic situation, and soon you'll feel sad, maybe even begin to cry. The thought itself motivates your body to participate.

One who decides to gain more happiness and peace of mind, and embarks on the career of seeking the good in all things and all people, will find what he is looking for. Just thinking about it makes it happen.

> *Happy are those who sit in Your house [Hashem]; they shall continue to praise You forever.*
>
> (Tehillim 84:5)

Sitting in the House of Hashem is a step in the right direction. It sets the mood. It gives you the impetus to want to sing along and learn the songs of Torah and mitzvos.

By your decision to be happy, Hashem causes your body to relax and achieve an optimal hormonal balance. Your glands will produce the hormones that cause the greatest benefits. Thus, happiness is in the mind and from the mind.

The *Shulchan Aruch* (*Orach Chaim* 231) devotes a chapter to the subject of doing everything for the sake of Heaven (*Avos* 2:17). This is a halachic obligation, like any other law of the *Shulchan Aruch*. But how does this work? Are we not merely deceiving ourselves by saying before a meal, "I will eat now for the sake of Hashem"?

The answer is that it will become true eventually. Your thoughts, your focus, and your desire causes a reaction from within.

Opposition

How does one deal with opposition? You may be eager, willing, and determined to do whatever it takes, but your coworkers, spouse, customers, or boss may have different ideas. How does Hashem assist you, if other people are opposing you?

You may have considered the following question: There are people in my life who always seem to be doing things wrong and then blaming me for it. Why does that happen to me? How can I bring to their attention that they are guilty of shifting their blame to me? (Does Hashem pick on me or allow others to do so without reason?)

There is a fascinating concept, based on Koheles (7:14):

Hashem has made one thing opposite another.

The Gemara explains with a specific example:

Hashem created the righteous, and He created the wicked [to balance each other and the world].

(*Chagigah* 15a)

Hashem, Who created everything with the greatest amount of planning and purpose, designed all the phenomena of this world to cooperate with each other. There is a system of collaboration between every component of the world. For example, the sun raises water vapor from the oceans, which is then transported inland by the wind in the form of clouds. The force of gravity participates in assisting the rain to pour down and cause life to grow.

Similarly, the righteous and wicked are linked together. How and why? Hashem does not compel anyone to be good or otherwise. The fundamental principle of free will is that Hashem does not generally interfere with a person's choices, although He foresees what a person will choose (Rambam, *Hilchos Teshuvah* 5:5). Hashem arranges challenges for each person in order to help promote his use of free will. Thus, the wicked are actually planted by Hashem to surround us, for our benefit.

The Talmud lists examples where the wicked help us:

> *Let Nimrod come and testify to the virtue of Avraham; Lavan will testify that Yaakov was 100 percent honest; the wife of Potifera will testify that Yosef was completely innocent from sin; Daryavesh will testify that Daniel never missed his prayers.*
>
> (*Avodah Zarah* 3a)

These examples are all eye-openers. (See Rav A. Miller's *Awake My Glory*, chap. 9, "The Wicked Make Us Great.") The wicked are placed by Hashem into a *tzaddik*'s life to test his piety to Hashem in all forms of perfection, including humility, patience, and kindliness. This is all part of Hashem's unique assistance program to help those who seek to purify themselves.

1) Avraham was the second greatest man in history. (Moshe was the greatest.) We are all considered

disciples of Avraham (*Avos* 5:19). He founded our nation and thus is called the pillar of the world (Rambam). But who helped motivate Avraham? A powerful tyrant who challenged him to a point where he even had him thrown into a fiery furnace. These tests helped develop Avraham's greatness.

2) Yaakov had to deal with a strong competitor from birth. At every step in life, he was forced to contend with his brother, Eisav. Subsequently, Lavan helped to perfect him. For twenty long years, he was tested by his father-in-law, Lavan, whose meanness and dishonesty was an ongoing ordeal. Yaakov passed his ordeal with flying colors and served Lavan continuously with all of his strength (Bereishis 31:6).

Yaakov had to constantly break his spirit of pride and anger as offerings to Hashem. For this, he was named Yisrael, "because you conquered angels and people" (Bereishis 32:39).

3) Daniel was stuck at a king's palace. Yet Scripture testifies that three times a day he would pray by his window, which faced Yerushalayim, as he had always done before despite the royal decree (Daniel 6:11). This was a fulfillment of the teaching in Tehillim (55:18): "In the evenings, morning, and noontime, I

speak and cry out [to Hashem], and He hears my voice."

A landlord, tenant, competitor, neighbor, spouse, coworker, or in-law who seems to cause you trouble is actually put in your life for your benefit. Hashem has arranged for them to test you and help you become great.

"Everything is in the Hands of Heaven..." (*Berachos* 33b) and "whatever the Merciful One does is for good" (*Berachos* 60b) are the keys to understanding all opposition. Difficult people and difficult situations are planned for our benefit. When we choose to respond in the most appropriate manner possible, we gain perfection and find favor in Hashem's eyes.

Now we understand the answer to our original question: The rule of "in the way one is determined to go he is led" includes Hashem positioning people in our lives for the purpose of assisting us in our goals. *Sanhedrin* 37a proclaims: "Each person is obligated to realize and say, 'The world was created for Me!' "

The Best Response

Although one can be aware of the fact that those who oppose us are here for our benefit, it is hard to take control of ourselves in order to deal with them.

The best approach to dealing with opposition is to respond with courtesy and warmth (instead of reacting with irritation and anger):

Who is to be honored? He who honors others.

(*Avos* 4:1)

Our Sages teach:

How beloved are human beings, for they are created in the image of Hashem!

(*Avos* 3:18)

Thus, even a person who is minimally righteous is more important than everything else in the universe. All of Creation was justified for the existence of even a single person. There is a portion of the Divine soul in every human being, which was implanted by the Creator. Keeping this in mind will help us respond properly to opposition.

Similarly, the Mishnah declares:

How beloved is the Jewish nation, for they are called the children of Hashem...

(Ibid.)

Jews specifically are obligated to "love your fellow man as yourself" (VaYikra 19:18), a mitzvah which is considered the most inclusive concept of the entire Torah (*Shabbos* 31a).

When the Choice Is Right

In the way one is determined to go he is led.

(*Makkos* 10b)

When Hashem is pleased with the ways of a person, even his enemies will make peace with him.

(Mishlei 16:7)

We can undestand now that these two sources complement each other:

1) Hashem leads a person on the path he is determined to go.

2) If that path is the right one (i.e., Hashem is pleased with the person's choice), Hashem causes all of that person's opposition to cease in order to assist him, or, alternately, Hashem provides certain forms of opposition to assist in promoting ultimate success of the endeavor.

Thus, one who finds himself faced with opposition should ask himself:

1) Am I on the right track?

2) Am I willing to make the commitment and efforts necessary to succeed in this endeavor with the help of Hashem?

3) Is it time for me to review the guidelines the *Chovos HaLevavos* teaches in his section on *bitachon* (chap. 4) regarding how to deal with other people?

These guidelines are:

1) When you need a favor, realize that Hashem is the Ultimate Provider and that this person (the opposition) may be Hashem's messenger for now. If you are successful, thank Hashem and the agent. If you do not seem to succeed now, thank Hashem for choosing not to grant what you thought you needed for the time being, and thank the agent for his time and efforts.

2) When someone blames you for something you think you are not guilty of:

  a) Trust in Hashem, Who knows the truth.

  b) Do not take revenge.

  c) Focus on Mishlei (12:21): "No harm will befall a *tzaddik*." No one can harm you or help you without Hashem's decree.

  d) Consider that Hashem may be causing this person to oppose you in order to motivate you to repent and ask Hashem for forgiveness, and thus

cause you to improve your ways so that Hashem
will then change your enemies into friends.

As long as your choice is right, you can be sure
Hashem is assisting you — even with opposition.

Accelerating Results

How does Hashem fulfill His part to assist us
when we are fully committed?

...One mitzvah leads to another.

(*Avos* 4:2)

When we perform a mitzvah, even a seemingly
minor one, we unleash a spiritual chain reaction that
drags us to other mitzvah opportunities. To begin is
the difficult part. After that, Hashem has many ways
of providing us with assistance. For example, you
may be determined to raise a million dollars for a
mitzvah project. As you solidify your commitment,
the money begins to come in. Soon things move faster
and faster until you succeed.

Hashem may test your commitment at the beginning to verify your determination. Then, when
Hashem decides to help you, all sorts of things may
occur. A whole stream of events may develop from
your decision. Unforeseen incidents, serendipitous

meetings, and material assistance will materialize to help you toward your goal.

On the path one is determined to go he will be led.

Seven-Step Formula

Let us conclude this section with a summary based on the seven-word Hebrew formula for guaranteed success:

בדרך, "on the path": Once a day, while walking down a road or path, ask yourself: Do I have a clear goal that I am aiming for? What is my primary goal in life? What do I keep praying to Hashem for? (See Tehillim 27:4.)

שאדם, "that a person": The significance of the description *"adam,"* the name Hashem used to identify man (see Bereishis 5:2), reminds us of the rare opportunity which our body (originally of earth) presents to us. While his soul is in his body, a person has the gift of free will with which to achieve virtue and perfection. The purpose of being alive is to use our life to serve Hashem, as by singing His praises (Tehillim 146:2). This should be our foremost goal — choosing to serve Him with our free will.

רוצה, "desires": The key is to develop a burning desire. "One thing I have been asking of Hashem; that is what I shall always seek..." (Tehillim 27:4). Thinking that you desire many objectives is a fallacy, because your focus is diluted when it is spread thin. Always asking Hashem for the same goal and striving to achieve it sincerely is the key.

Making a decision that you *should* change is not enough. Knowing that you *will* change someday is also not enough. The guarantee of our Sages is dependent on developing a sense of urgency that is so intense that you are *compelled* to follow through immediately, with the help of Hashem.

לילך, "to go": Make a solid decision to take action now. You should be at the roadside with your shoes on, shoelaces tied, ready to go.

בו, "in it": The commitment has to be focused in an exclusive manner: no options, no alternatives. The wealthiest man in America today is said to have excelled even as a boy in his determination. He was so focused on his goals that it took him wherever he wanted to go.

מוליכין, "they will lead": Without Divine assistance, it is impossible to succeed (*Kiddushin* 30b): "If I am not for myself who will be for me? When I am for

myself, what am I [without the help of Hashem]?"
(*Avos* 1:14).

אותו, "him": "He" will succeed. To do so, a person
must condition his mind to visualize his success. "I
requested one thing of Hashem that I continue to seek:
to sit in the house of Hashem all the days of my life,
to view the delights..." (Tehillim 27).

On the path one is determined to go he will be led!

TWO

Prayer

Ask for It

Open your mouth wide, and I will fill it.

(Tehillim 81:11)

This passage refers to Hashem urging us to ask Him for our needs, and His promise to fulfill them. (We say this verse daily in the *"Hodu"* prayer, and on Thursdays, in the *Shir shel Yom* near the end of davening.) In other words, ask for what your heart desires, and Hashem will fulfill it.

What a treasure we have at our disposal! By asking Hashem for everything we need, we demonstrate our faith in Hashem's power and generosity, which is unlimited. This realization makes us worthy to have our prayers answered.

If it's so easy, why not just do it?

The reasons some find it hard to pray to Hashem:

1) Doesn't Hashem know our thoughts? Why do we have to spell it out?

2) What if we are rejected?

3) Does our pride stand in our way and block our willingness to ask Hashem for assistance?

4) Perhaps we are not worthy to ask and receive whatever we desire?

This section addresses these doubts, and we pray to Hashem for assistance in learning to overcome these barriers.

Whom to Ask

I am Hashem, your God, Who raised you up from the land of Egypt. Open your mouth wide, and I will fill it.

(Tehillim 81:11)

We all want happiness and fulfillment. We would like to live at our maximum potential with an ongoing sense of excitement and purpose. The big question, then, is how to achieve this goal.

The best and only answer is, with the help of Hashem. In this verse from Tehillim, we find Hashem urging us to open our mouths wide, i.e., to request of Him the unlimited perfection available to us. To us, this verse might seem strange. We are accustomed to people saying, "Don't bother me. I'm busy now." And when was the last time someone said to you, "Ask me for whatever you like?"

Hashem is different. He is unique. He created us, cares for us, and wishes to continue to guide us to achieve our utmost.

So ask!

Resistance

We are hesitant to ask. We find excuses. One of the primary excuses is "I am unworthy."

To counter this resistance, the verse begins with "I am Hashem, Your God, Who raised you up from the land of Egypt."

Hashem created you in His image. He made you special. He chose you to be one of His children. And He has demonstrated His unique love for you by performing countless miracles for you such as when He redeemed you from Egypt.

This means you are supremely worthy. Indeed, the Talmud teaches, "In every single generation a person is obligated to consider all the miracles of the Exodus as being done for him" (*Pesachim* 116b).

In studying the preface to this verse, we can learn to appreciate its conclusion: "Open your mouth wide, and I will fill it."

Yes, we are worthy.

Shame

One who is bashful will not learn.

(*Avos* 2:6)

One who is afraid to ask his rebbe to clarify his teachings will remain in doubt.

(*Bartenura* loc. cit.)

Similarly, one who is reluctant to ask Hashem for his needs will remain with an empty mouth. Hashem is teaching us that He will wait until we open our mouths wide to Him before He will fill it up.

Prayer has been called the world's most powerful and neglected secret to success and happiness. If only we would open our mouths we would be answered.

So don't be afraid! Just ask.

However, there is a legitimate concern, which Mishlei (28:9) refers to: "He who refuses to listen to Torah, his prayers are also an abomination." The reason for this is that Hashem may say, If you are unwilling to listen to Me, why should I listen to you? To remedy this, we must be willing to listen to Him.

How to Ask

The most fascinating part about this subject is that Hashem wants us to know how He will respond before we even ask Him for help. Hashem urges us, "Open your mouth wide, and I will fill it."

How do you ask for something if you are sure that your needs will be met with abundance? Your posture, your eyes, your tone of voice, and choice of words are all geared to following the rules.

What are the rules? *Shulchan Aruch* (98:3) states: "One should pray as a pauper at the door requesting a handout — with gentle entreaties."

This method, which is called *"derech tachanunim,"* is explained to mean the following: The seeker expresses his powerful desire to find favor with Hashem although he is undeserving (*Praise My Soul*, paragraph 1289).

The *Mishnah Berurah* explains (98:3): Focus on the fact that no mortal, angel, *mazal*, or star can help you without the will of Hashem. You need Hashem to have mercy on you. It is all up to Hashem.

We are taught to imagine that Hashem is desperately eager, so to speak, to provide us with that which we request of Him. To fortify our conviction, the *pasuk* begins with Who Hashem is and His track record. He is the Creator and the Controller of the universe. He saved us from Egypt and elevated us by giving us His Torah. Thus He has the power to provide you with what you need or want.

The expression "I am Hashem, your God" means not only in the past but forever. I am your God Who cares for you with a special love. As we find emphasized in Tehillim (117:2), His kindliness to us is overwhelming.

This preface also leads to another fundamental point. What type of assistance is Hashem most interested in providing? He has elevated us to greatness in order to serve Him. Thus the Gemara explains, "This verse refers specifically to matters of Torah" (*Berachos* 50a). When we ask Him for assistance in Torah study, He is most eager to respond with abundance.

Does this mean we should not ask Him for money? The answer is that the Gemara is referring to opening one's mouth wide, i.e., asking for super-abundance. We should be reserved when asking for materialistic needs. Ask for five million dollars instead of ten. However, when it comes to spiritual goals, we should go all out and pray for abundant success. Also, our material needs are essential only in order for us to be able to serve Hashem. "If there is no food, there will be no Torah" (*Avos* 3:17). Thus, we should pray for sustenance in abundance, so that we can study Torah in an abundant manner.

Gently

The *Shulchan Aruch* (98:3) adds, "[Pray] gently."

Ask Hashem in a gentle manner. Imagine asking a person for a favor in a harsh tone of voice: "Give me that!"

Now try: "You are always so thoughtful and generous. Please help me now, too." (See how we begin Shemoneh Esreh in the siddur.)

A person must always set forth the praises of Hashem before asking his requests.

(*Berachos* 32a)

We acknowledge His greatness and wisdom before we entreat Him to hearken to our prayer. People are much more prone to help us if we are friendly, considerate, and polite to them. If we respect and admire them sincerely, they are more willing to listen.

A parent teaches a child, "Say 'please'!" Hashem teaches us the same.

Ask for Specifics

We specify and enumerate our needs to Hashem in our prayers. When we ask for intelligence in Shemoneh Esreh, we do not pray for one general request. Rather, we ask for (1) knowledge, (2) understanding, and (3) wisdom.

(To understand the difference between these three is a study in itself, which we should undertake and for which we should also pray to Hashem.)

Similarly, when we conclude the Shemoneh Esreh with a request for peace, we also list its subdivisions: (1) goodness and blessing, (2) favor and kindliness, and (3) mercy.

Why do we specify?

Chovos HaLevovos (*Cheshbon HaNefesh* 18) explains: "Hashem knows exactly what we need before we say anything. However, He wants us to realize how much we need Him and have to depend on Him." When we do our part, "Open your mouth wide," and specify, He will answer. This also explains why it is essential to pray with sincere feelings. If you don't really mean what you are saying, you are not fooling anyone. Hashem sees right through you! We must pray with persistence until we finally understand how much we need Him for every one of our prayers.

Some specifics one can ask for are:

Someone to listen to you, to provide you with the attention you need, to care for you, to respect you, and to teach you how to understand your prayers. You can pray for someone who will help you around the house, information, help in raising and educating your children, help with a project, for others to cooperate with you, or for car-pool help. You can pray for wealth, fame, or to lose weight. You can ask for a loan, better terms on a loan, a raise, to be able to pay your bills, or to be able to pay full tuition. The list is endless...

Keep Asking

If a person sees that his prayers were not answered, let him pray again. As it says: "Hope to Hashem; be

*strong and fortify yourself, and hope to Hashem
[again]" (Tehillim 27:14).*

(Berachos 32b)

Don't put all your "begs" in one "ask-for-it." By
asking Hashem repeatedly for something, eventually
you learn to mean what you say.

This lesson may also be included in our original
verse "Open your mouth wide," not only once, but
keep on opening it up with prayers to Hashem.

Hashem's "no" may be merely a "you're not ready
for it yet." Yitzchak and Rivkah prayed for children
for twenty years (Bereishis 25:21; see *The Beginning*, p.
396). This means they entreated Hashem with fervent
prayers, tears, and outcries all that time. They engaged in lengthy and vigorous prayers, which served
as an ongoing training program of awareness and
devotion to Hashem.

An author, whose book was rejected by twenty-six
publishers, wrote that each time he would call to find
out what the problem was and how he could improve
his chances. He then made the suggested changes they
pointed out. He began to look forward to rejections in
order to improve his work. Thus the twenty-seventh
publisher who bought the work received a manu-

script that had benefited from the advice of twenty-six professionals.

Priorities

Imagine if we were to receive a signed blank check from the Bank of Heaven and were urged to fill it in for the amount of our choice.

Near the beginning of Shlomo HaMelech's career, Hashem made him such an offer:

Ask for what you would like Me to give you.

(Melachim I 3:5)

Shlomo could have requested longevity, wealth, or power (see Melachim I 3:11), but he chose a wise and understanding heart.

However, there was a surprising result to this episode. Hashem's response included the following:

And also that which you did not request I have bestowed upon you: wealth and power...

(Ibid. 3:13)

Hashem's offer to Shlomo is reminiscent of the offer in Tehillim, "Open your mouth wide, and I will fill it." With the surprising results to Shlomo HaMelech, we can understand our verse better. Rashi interprets "Open your mouth wide" as meaning, "Ask Me for all that your heart desires."

"And I will fill it" — I shall fulfill your every request. Rashi seems to ignore the *gemara* (*Berachos* 50a) which explains the *pasuk* to refer only to matters of Torah. The Targum, however, solves this question: "Open your mouth wide in words of Torah, and I will fill it with everything good."

The concept here may be the same as by Shlomo HaMelech. When you ask for the right things, you deserve much more. By asking for Torah, you also receive that which will enable you to study Torah. You get the whole package deal.

You may not get what you ask for; you may get much more!

Benefits of Prayer

1) *You enhance your status.* The Talmud (according to Rav, *Bava Kama* 3b) defines man as "*maveh,*" the one who prays. The art of prayer is what distinguishes a person more than any other endeavor. Animals can fight, build houses, or live in communities like people. But to address the Creator of the universe and to speak to Him in first person, so to speak, is something that only people can do (*Alei Shur*, p. 27).

2) *You develop your trait of chesed.* Concentrating in prayer is included in the trait of *gemilus chasadim* because it develops one's *nefesh* (Rashi, *Shabbos* 127b).

3) *You develop profound awareness.* The Ramban (*Shemos* 3:13) declares: The greatest proof that Hashem is with us all the time is that He responds to our prayer requests at all times!

To stimulate prayer, Hashem even sends misfortune upon people in order to cause them to pray more. But not everyone is worthy of these special promotions, only the righteous.

The Talmud (*Yevamos* 64a) relates: Why did our ancestors have difficulty having children? Because Hashem desires the prayers of the righteous.

Every prayer is an opportunity to realize that we are in the presence of Hashem. When we speak to Hashem urgently and address Him with the direct "You" as our prayers require, and we stand before Him and bow down to Him, we learn to experience the sensation of speaking to Hashem.

The eyes of all [the living] hope to You, and You give them their food in its time.

(Tehillim 145:15)

Why didn't Hashem arrange the world so that we would find large supplies of food like we find minerals? Why do we always need to plant and grow food?

This system helps even the wealthy to constantly pray to Hashem for new supplies of food in order to always be mindful of Him.

Who Is Asking?

This incredible verse should be ringing in our ears: "Open your mouth wide, and I will fill it." Is it logical? Just like that, Hashem will provide whatever you desire?

Chovos HaLevavos (*Bitachon* 3) states: The fourth premise of *bitachon* is to pay attention and invest effort to fulfill that which the Creator requires of you. *Bitachon* does not mean trust in Hashem without logic. Rather, it is based on the awareness that Hashem alone is in complete control of everything. Therefore, in order to achieve what you desire from Him, exert yourself to gain Hashem's favor with the hope that Hashem will favor you in His great kindness because of your behavior and prayers.

This concept is obvious in many sources, such as chapter 37 of Tehillim, verses 1–5:

1) Do not imitate the wicked; do not envy the evildoers.

2) For like grass they will quickly disappear...

3) Trust in Hashem and do good deeds...

4) And you will merit to delight in Hashem, for He will grant your desires...

5) Turn over your needs to Hashem, and trust in Him and He will produce.

This helps us to understand better the verse we started with:

1) "I am Hashem your God" — Do you realize the truth of this fact? Do you behave in a manner that demonstrates your understanding of this basic truth?

2) "Who raised you up from the land of Egypt" — I have always been helping you and will continue to do so, if you are interested.

3) "Open your mouth wide, and I will fill it" — You must ask for your needs with the realization of Who I am and what I have done for you. Then you will deserve a guaranteed response.

The answer is yes...but you have to ask!

Truth in Asking

1) Do you truly desire that which you are requesting from Hashem?

2) Are you convinced that only Hashem can help you?

3) Are you doing your part to deserve Hashem's aid?

4) Are you paying attention to the prayers you are reciting?

These four questions are based on Rav Avigdor Miller's commentary on the siddur (*Praise My Soul*, pp. 404–408), where he explains four aspects in understanding the following verse from "*Ashrei*":

> *Hashem is close to all those who call Him, to all who call Him in truth!*

1) One who requests of Hashem to supply him with his livelihood and other needs but makes no effort to obtain them demonstrates the weakness and insincerity of his request.

2) When a person who requests health or life is careless with his health or reckless with his life, his prayers are lacking in sincerity.

3) One who prays for success in Torah learning must demonstrate his sincerity by toiling in Torah study. One who seeks to improve himself and fulfill the great mitzvah of repentance, or to develop his *emunah* with the profound knowledge of the Torah's

teachings, must apply himself to the study of Torah and *mussar*.

One who really desires something will commit himself to attempt to achieve it. At the same time, it is essential to be convinced that one's own efforts are in vain unless Hashem favors them. To gain Hashem's favor, you have to exert yourself to keep His laws; follow His requirements, obligations, and precepts; and beware of His prohibitions.

A simple test to determine your preparedness for sincere prayer would be to ask yourself the following questions:

1) Am I willing to do whatever it takes to accomplish this goal?

2) Does Hashem want me to do whatever it takes to accomplish this?

If the answers are negative, why? Are there other factors that need to be taken into consideration? If so, factor them in, and then ask yourself the questions again.

(A reminder for this concept would be the acronym WITH: Whatever It Takes, with the *H* for Hashem.)

What to Ask For

What do you ask Hashem for most? What is your purpose in life? What would you do if you knew that Hashem would help you succeed? What would you be, and how would you do it if you could be anything you chose to be?

These questions can change your life. Ask them of yourself over and over again. Think about them for a few weeks. Focus on praying to Hashem for help in formulating an answer and applying it.

Let us study some answers from the Gemara (*Berachos* 8a) to the question, What should I pray for?

For this, let every pious person pray to You at a time of happening...

(Tehillim 32:6)

What does "this" refer to?

A shidduch: A person may find the right one, a pious and wise woman, but then reject her without realizing that she is more precious than great wealth (Mishlei 31:10). We must pray for help from Hashem to get it right. This also includes ongoing prayers to Hashem for marital peace and harmony for those who are fortunate to be married.

Torah: This includes finding the right *chavrusa*, the right rebbe, the right time for a daily Torah-study session, to study the entire *Talmud Bavli* and *Yerushalmi* with all of the commentaries and *poskim*... " 'Open your mouth wide [i.e., request the utmost], and I will fill it' (Tehillim 81:11) — this refers to Torah study" (*Berachos* 50a). This also includes prayers for help in reviewing one's Torah studies constantly.

Long life: To die of old age and in a gentle manner. We pray, "Teach us to count our days wisely, so that we bring wisdom into our hearts" (Tehillim 90:12). Learning wisdom is the purpose of life, and we must pray fervently to accomplish this.

Peace: We sum up our Shemoneh Esreh with a blessing for peace, because it encompasses everything else: health and peace of mind (internal peace); no wars, litigation, or marital strife (external peace); and prosperity (financial peace).

Health: We pray that we don't get disease, headaches, toothaches, insanity...

These five areas form the general outline of our prayers in life. For each of these areas, we need extensive prayer throughout our lifetime, the more the better. As an example for prayers for Torah study, there are many *sefarim* and tapes that can change your life for the better. There are *sefarim* that can help you succeed in your career. There are Torah guidebooks that can help you improve your marriage and your child-raising capacity. But how often do you merit to find the right *sefer* for your particular needs?

It has been said that if you would study a *sefer* a month in any chosen field, you would become one of the top experts in that field in about five years. But how many people pray for such success?

To decide which topic is of special interest to you, you can also pray for assistance.

When to Ask

Don't wait! If you wait until the weather is just right, you will never plant or harvest your crops (see Koheles 11:4).

We pray before we set out and thereafter at frequent intervals for everything we wish to do. The more we request of Hashem, the more we come to feel that everything depends solely on Him, and thus we become closer to Him.

When do I become beloved to Hashem? When He hears the voice of my entreaties.

(*Pesachim* 118b)

Before taking a morning walk, we request Hashem's help for all that we need, including that He open our eyes in order to notice His marvelous creations (*Sing, You Righteous*, p. 285).

Jewish Mothers

Jewish mothers have always prayed from their hearts, whenever they found a few moments. They have a prayer for every eventuality: on rising, on going to bed, for an unwell child, for a child to remain on the right path, that her husband should earn a livelihood, that Hashem should help His people. When lighting the Shabbos candles, she prays that her husband, children, and grandchildren illuminate the world like the Shabbos candles and become righteous Torah scholars and that her daughters be worthy to merit marrying such Jews (*Awake My Glory*, p. 347).

Every step, stratagem, and undertaking must be prefaced with a prayer to Hashem for success.

Our soul hopes to Hashem; He is our help and shield.

(Tehillim 33:20)

Despite our energetic efforts, we look solely to Him to make our plans for success prosper ("He is our help") and to make our precautions against misfortune effective ("He is our shield") (*Awake My Glory*, p. 372).

Prayer Maxims

- Put your prayer where your mouth and heart is.

- An ounce of prayer is worth a pound of cure.

- Determination plus goal-setting plus concentration plus prayer equals success.

- Prayer transforms
  a stumbling block into a steppingstone,
  a problem into a pearl,
  a peril into a prize.

- Prayer promotes performance.

- A weak prayer attitude can undermine all positive skills.

- Arrogance is deadly, for it short-circuits the desire for sincere prayer to Hashem.

- You're not praying when you're talking!

- It's your choice every day to daven better.

- The opportunity for sincere prayer comes at unexpected times.

- Pray harder with more concentration.

- Prayer without action is incomplete.
- The best defense is a good prayer.
- Tell the truth in prayer.
- Be serious about your prayers.
- Never take your prayers for granted.
- If you are not changing, you are not praying.
- Stop, listen, and think before you pray.
- Your chances for success increases in proportion to the number of prayer calls you make to Hashem.
- Have an objective for every prayer.
- One who prays to Hashem is succeeding in life.
- One who prays has hope; one who has hope has everything.
- Prayer with sincerity is the first principle of success.
- You can do it if you pray for assistance.
- If you don't know what you are praying for, what do you think you will receive?
- Take time to recharge your prayer batteries.
- Your prayers are a virtue. Don't give up.
- A failure prays only once; a winner keeps on praying.

- It's better to pray too much than too little.
- If you think you can pray and succeed, you are right.
- Prayer is the root of all success.
- Prayer to Hashem is the greatest honor!
- Whether you are rich or poor, prayer is essential.
- The best time to pray for something is before you need it.
- Opportunity knocks each time you pray to Hashem.
- Every path has its prayer.
- A prayer well stated is a problem solved.
- Prayer to Hashem is the best and safest course.
- Without prayer, all other virtues lose their value.
- Nothing besides prayer to Hashem can guide you as well in life.
- Pray ahead to get ahead.
- Ninety-five percent of success is prayer.
- The more you pray, the more you receive.
- You never fail with prayer. Each prayer is a positive result.
- Every obstacle is an opportunity for prayer.

- Prevent spiritual decay: pray with feeling every day.

- Your prayer budget is more important than your financial one.

- Life is what happens to you in response to your prayers.

- The more you pray, the more you profit.

- Pray that you learn how to give but never how to give up.

- Winning isn't everything; prayer to win is.

- With prayer no one will fail; without it no one will succeed.

- If it ain't broke, pray it doesn't break.

- Nothing is impossible with prayer; everything is impossible without it.

- It's always safe to pray for others.

- Guard your prayers, and your prayers will guard you.

- The greatest of all abilities is the power to pray.

- A person becomes what he prays for most of the time.

- Pray all you can; it is a most powerful strength.

- Prayer is a priceless gift, a key that opens one's life.
- Prayer is our toll-free number to Hashem.
- The starting point of all achievement is prayer.
- As you master the art of prayer, you master all else.
- Whatever the problem, prayer is the solution.
- Don't believe in miracles — pray for them.
- The only ones who fail are those who fail to pray.

Prayer Facts

- A lesson from children: When they want something they turn to their parents and cry.
- Your only real limitations are those for which you fail to pray.
- Statistic: 50,000 Americans become blind each year; that is about 1 every 10 minutes. The need for prayer is urgent. We must thank Hashem sincerely for the gift of vision daily, and also pray that we enjoy this gift for 120 years.
- When you buy something, it's not really money you are spending; it is time and prayer.
- Marriages are made in Heaven, but a lot of the details have to be prayed for here on earth.

- The most important safety preparations of all are prayers to Hashem to protect us from all danger.

- You can make more friends in a week by praying for help from Hashem than by trying on your own for a year.

- The starting point of all achievement is a prayer to Hashem for assistance.

- When you consider something "impossible," you are obviously not taking into account the power of prayer.

- Change the notion "Change is the only constant" to "Prayer is the only constant."

- It's not what you know or who you know — it's what you pray for to Hashem that makes the difference.

- It's not what happens to you, but how you pray for what happens that makes the difference.

- You're not old until you run out of prayers.

- Great opportunities for unusual prayers are infrequent; but small, steady prayer opportunities surround us daily.

- Early prayers can save your life!

- Everything is achieved by one who prays while waiting.

- Prayer is the superglue of life. It can repair anything.

- There are no limits on our future if we don't put limits on our prayers.

- Prayer is language at its most powerful state.

- Moments of sincere prayer literally create memories of a lifetime.

- Prayer is the rent you pay for a room on Hashem's earth.

Prayer Counts

- It's not only the thought that counts; it's also the prayers that make the difference!

- The difference between stumbling blocks and steppingstones is the resulting prayers!

- It's not what you pray for that holds you back; it's what you do not pray for.

- It's what you say in prayer, as much as the way you say it, that counts.

- No one has more hours each day than you do. Pray that you use your time wisely.

- You are not what you think you are; you are what you pray for.

- It's not what you are planning to do that counts; it's what you are planning to pray for.

- The will to pray is not much without the will to prepare for prayer.

- It's not where you start; it's what you pray for that counts.

- To be an overnight success requires about twenty years of prayer.

Prayer Benefits

Prayer is good for your health. It helps the body's immune system, cures depression, reduces stress, induces sleep, invigorates, rejuvenates your entire system without unpleasant side effects. It is nothing less than a miracle drug. It is all-natural, organic, sweet, without pesticides, preservatives, or artificial ingredients. It is 100 percent wholesome. You do not have to worry about moveable parts or batteries wearing out (except to keep your siddur and Tehillim in good shape). It requires low-energy consumption and produces a high-energy yield. It is inflation-proof and non-fattening. No monthly payments or insurance requirements. It is theft-proof, non-taxable, non-polluting, and fully guaranteed by the Highest Authority.

Prayer Goals

- Prayer is essential for every goal in life. Specific prayers are available for various goals, such as:

    1) For security (Tehillim 27).

    2) For financial needs (Tehillim 37).

    3) For a boost at work (Tehillim 128).

    4) For aid when travelling (Tehillim 121).

- The purpose of prayer is to make yourself *think*! (Rav A. Miller).

- The purpose of life is to serve Hashem. One of the best forms of service to Him is prayer.

- Pray for everything, including peace of mind, health, energy, loving relationships, financial success, worthy goals and ideals, self-knowledge, and personal fulfillment.

- Pray for assistance in being honest, intelligent, responsible, organized, committed, focused on priorities, disciplined, enthusiastic, positive, cheerful, decisive, competent, energized, and determined in the service of Hashem.

- Pray to buy a house and turn it into a home;
  to buy a bed and get a good night's sleep;
  to achieve true pleasure and happiness;
  to have genuine good times with peace of mind;
  to have companions who are also friends.

Prayer Power

- Prayer to Hashem is power.

- It costs nothing yet creates so much!

- It enriches those whom we pray for without impoverishing those who pray.

- It requires little time, and the effect can be everlasting.

- No one is too wealthy to get along without it; and no one is too poor to be enriched by its benefits.

- It creates happiness in the home, goodwill in business, and lasting friendships.

- It energizes the weary, the discouraged, the sad, and those in trouble.

- The supply is unlimited.

- Prayer pushes away fear.

- It helps atone for sins.

- It is an invincible power.

- There is no difficulty that enough prayer will not conquer, no disease that enough prayer will not heal, no door that prayer will not open.

- With prayer, you can be the happiest and most powerful person in the world.

- Prayer is more powerful than money, mightier than a sword.

Prayer Skills

- Learn how to pray with concentration, as if your life depends on it — because it does.

- We are all born with the potential ability to pray well. However, we tend to fail to develop this skill.

- Learn to control your mind and heart while praying, and you will have a powerful tool at your disposal.

- Pray for at least one new item per day.

- Never be too busy to pray for small things.

- Pray for yourself. Only you know what you really need.

- Begin and close your day with prayer.

- Ask Hashem to help you. His help is the only one that truly matters.

Prayers and Answers

You may ask for strength to achieve;
Hashem may cause weakness to teach humility.
You may ask for health to do great things;
He may send infirmity so that you do better things.
You may ask for riches to be happy;
He may send poverty to make you wise.
You may ask for power to gain recognition from others;
He may give you weakness so that you learn that you need Him.
You may ask for all things to enjoy life;
He may give you life to enjoy all things.

He knows how to answer all your prayers for your ultimate benefit.

Successful Prayers

- All success begins and ends with a prayer.

- All prayer is based on positive belief. "Hashem desires those who fear Him, those who hope for His kindliness" (Tehillim 147).

- With prayer, a person can focus and develop a driving force to overcome all obstacles. "In the way one wishes to go he is led" (*Makkos* 10b).

- Use the three *P*'s: Prayer, Patience, and Persistence.

- Planning and prayer are essential. "A wise person foresees the future" (*Tamid* 32a).

- Don't settle for less. "Open your mouth wide [in prayer and desire], and I will fill it" (Tehillim 81).

Prayer Thoughts

- Do I pray for myself — or do I merely follow the masses and pray routinely?

- Put yourself in another's place; picture yourself there, and then you can begin to pray for him/her.

- If you pray long enough and with enough thought you are sure to wake yourself up.

- Sometimes we are so busy praying to make a living that we forget to pray for life!

- People begin to pray when they decide to. Now is the time.

- When you begin to pray, your world will begin to shape up.

- Your success, health, happiness, and wealth depend on how you pray.

- You can always pray to become the person you would have liked to be!

THREE

Learning to Laugh
with Rabbi Akiva

Training to Laugh

In order to succeed in life, a person must develop the capacity to laugh. We are referring here to a specific form of laughter, an attitude that stems from a mitzvah:

> *A person must always train himself to say, "All that the Merciful One does is for good!"*
> (*Shulchan Aruch, Orach Chaim* 230:5)

The source of this halachah is the Talmudic teaching in the name of Rabbi Akiva. Let us begin by studying the source and the illustration that is cited there:

> *Rabbi Akiva came to a city during one of his travels. He sought lodgings, but he was refused. His reaction: "All that the Merciful One does is for good" [i.e., there is definitely a benefit for me in this seeming difficulty that Hashem is causing].*
>
> *So he went to sleep in a field. With him he had his rooster [to wake him up early], his donkey [for travel], and a candle.*
>
> *A gust of wind extinguished his light, a wild cat ate his rooster, and a lion attacked and devoured his donkey. His response: "All that the Merciful One does is for good."*
>
> *That night, a band of robbers captured the town that had refused him lodgings. He then told his disciples: "Didn't I tell you, 'All that the Holy One, blessed be He, does is all for good'?"*
>
> (Berachos 60b)

Had the candle been lit, they may have seen me. If the donkey would have brayed or the rooster crowed, they would have captured me, too.

*So why did Hashem give me four difficulties, lack
of lodging, lack of light, lack of an animal, and lack
of a bird? To save my life!*

(*Rashi*)

What to Say

Why did Rabbi Akiva keep saying, "All that the
Merciful One does is for good"?

Perhaps he was obligated to do so in thankfulness
for the benefits he was receiving. (If you received
valuable gifts, wouldn't you be thankful and express
your gratitude for each one?) Perhaps he was also
training himself to have a deeper and more concrete
feeling of appreciation and love of Hashem for everything Hashem was doing for him.

The bottom line is that this approach is cited in
Shulchan Aruch (see above) as a way of life for all of
us!

To make this a part of *your* way of life, here are
some suggestions:

1) Learn the ten Hebrew and Aramaic words of
this passage from the original source (*Berachos* 60b)
and memorize them. Then practice saying them fifty
times by heart until they become fluent in your mouth
and mind.

2) Contemplate some current examples of this phenomenon (people being saved by means of seeming misfortune) and relate them to this teaching of Rabbi Akiva.

Is there a minimum amount of required or suggested frequency for saying this phrase?

We can refer to Rabbi Akiva's teaching in *Sanhedrin* 99a–b: " '*Zemer*' every day." Rashi explains: "Keep organizing and reviewing your studies even after you are fluent in them, as in a song, so that you will merit joy and song in the World to Come."

The Key

Rabbi Akiva was one of the greatest Sages of all time. There are numerous incidents related about him and his teachings throughout the Talmud and Midrash. As we study these sources, it appears that this giant personality, whose greatness was exceptional and extraordinary in many ways, had a unique system.

B'ezras Hashem, we plan to suggest in this section that the above opening lesson — his teaching to react with optimism to all situations — is the key to many of his other teachings and qualities.

Caution

Before we embark on learning to laugh with Rabbi Akiva, it is necessary to point out that a balance is required. Rabbi Akiva did not overdo it. As a matter of fact, he teaches in *Pirkei Avos* (3:17): "Laughter and lightheadedness lead to immorality," which means that one should develop a serious, businesslike attitude in order to be protected from frivolity and sin.

A person must learn when to react with laughter and when to be serious. Both reactions have their time and place. Even before Rabbi Akiva became a Torah giant, when Rachel noticed his exceptional potential, she was amazed by his modesty and other exceptional qualities (*Kesubos* 62b). As he grew in Torah greatness he fine-tuned his potential to the dictates of the Torah.

Pan Am Flight 103

An outstanding example of Rabbi Akiva's "this is for good" theory has been openly demonstrated by the Hand of Heaven in an event which shocked the world.

Two hundred and seventy people were killed by an explosion on Pan Am flight 103. However, forty-three Jews scheduled to be on the flight missed it for various reasons. Some of them include:

- Some got stuck in traffic. (Did you ever think of saying, "Hashem has a good reason for traffic jams"?)

- One refused to board the plane because there did not seem to be enough Jews boarding to have a minyan for *minchah.*

- One transferred to an earlier flight in order to arrive early at his destination to perform a timely mitzvah. (A mitzvah can surely save your life!)

- One fellow got locked in an airport bathroom whose door jammed. (Sometimes Hashem uses unexpected ways to save people!)

Thus, each person who missed the plane should have been saying, "Hashem has caused me some benefit," even before he heard of the eventual crash.

Consider the Future

When a group of Sages walking along the road with Rabbi Akiva heard a tumult of idol worshippers, they began to weep; but Rabbi Akiva began to laugh.
They said to him: "Why are you laughing?"

He said to them: "Why are you weeping?"

They replied: "The idol worshippers are living seemingly carefree lives, while we are suffering from the destruction of the Beis HaMikdash. Is that not a cause for weeping?"

He answered: "That is my cause for laughter! Don't you realize that if a transgressor of Hashem's Torah receives some benefit, how much more will those who obey Hashem be rewarded?"

(Makkos 24a)

The same situation can be viewed in two ways:

1) The seemingly obvious — the wicked are rejoicing.

2) With Torah insight — who will rejoice more?

Opposite Reactions

Subsequently, these Sages were walking toward Yerushalayim. When they viewed the Temple site, they tore their garments [in mourning over the Destruction]. (Maharsha: Rabbi Akiva also tore his garments to mourn the Destruction and the loss of the Shechinah's Presence.)

When they arrived at the Temple site, they saw a fox exiting from the ruins of the Holy of Holies.

> *They began to weep. Rabbi Akiva began to laugh.*
> *They said to him: "Why are you laughing?"*
> *He replied: "Why are you weeping?"*
> *They said: "See the extent of the desolation! Even*
> *wild animals are roaming the area."*
>
> *He said: "That is why I laugh. As we can see, the*
> *prophecies of destruction are being fulfilled to the*
> *letter. We can thus be assured that the prophecies of*
> *the Redemption will also be fulfilled. Thus, this is the*
> *harbinger of good news."*
>
> *They said: "Akiva, you have consoled us! Akiva,*
> *you have consoled us!" (Maharsha: The repetition is*
> *a reference to both incidents.)*

> (Ibid.)

We see that the conclusion of the Sages was to accept Rabbi Akiva's approach. This coincides with the halachah we quoted previously that we are always required to say, "All that the Merciful One does is for good."

The Name

Why did the Sages call Rabbi Akiva by name at this point?

'   It may be that Rabbi Akiva's name itself symbol-
ized his approach. "Akiva" is a form of the name
"Yaakov." When Yaakov was born, the Torah
(Bereishis 25:26) says that he was holding the heel
(*eikev*) of Eisav. Thus, the name "Yaakov" signifies
that he is the one who will come at the end. His
ultimate success is in the future.

All Jews have a share in the World to Come.
                                                    (*Sanhedrin* 90a)

Thus, Rabbi Akiva taught: The good will be evident. It will reveal itself sooner or later. Hashem is
doing everything for our benefit. Even if we do not
uncover the hidden benefits in this world, we can be
sure that the ultimate time and place for Hashem's
perfect benevolence is the World to Come!

(In connection with this, we also note that Yaakov
was the son of Yitzchak, whose name means "he shall
laugh at the end." At the Final Redemption, we will
merit the fulfillment of "Then our mouths will be
filled with laughter" [Tehillim 126:2].)

How to Comfort Others

Why did the Sages use the word *"nechamah,"* which means comfort and consolation? (as in *nichum aveilim,* "comforting mourners").

We find in *Hilchos Aveilus* (*Yoreh De'ah* 376) specific halachos on what to say to comfort mourners. The *Aruch HaShulchan* (par. 5) says that one may say, "All that Hashem does is for good, and we have to accept Hashem's decree with love."

Thus we learn that this motto of Rabbi Akiva may be directed as a comfort not only to oneself but also to others.

In connection with comforting mourners, we will also study a selection from Rabbi Huna. (Although we are concentrating in this section on the teachings of Rabbi Akiva, it is worth noting that in the source in *Berachos* 60b the Gemara quotes the original teaching also in the name of Rabbi Huna in the name of Rav from Rabbi Meir.)

A woman in Rabbi Huna's neighborhood had seven sons. One of them passed away, causing her to grieve excessively. Rabbi Huna told her, "It is improper to overdo your grief." She disregarded his message. He then told her, "If you continue, you will need to prepare shrouds for your next son..."

There is an obligation to weep in mourning, but there is also an obligation to desist at the proper time.

Giving Is Getting

Included in the teaching that "all that the Merciful One does is for good," is the understanding that the entire Torah, which consists of Hashem's teachings, are all Good with a capital *G* — the Greatest of all Goods!

Thus we could take any mitzvah and show that it will benefit a person in numerous ways. As an example, we can ask, Is giving away money (for charity) good?

Rabbi Akiva answers this question in *Pirkei Avos* 3:17: "Giving *ma'aser* is a protection that [insures] one's wealth."

If you received a hundred dollars for each ten dollars you gave, would that be good or bad? We all accept the fact that *tzedakah* is a mitzvah we are obligated to fulfill. However, we are urged to develop the attitude of giving with a smile and the joyous realization that "it is for my benefit; I am also helping my-self."

Our Sages say, "Tithe [*aser*] so that you will become wealthy [*osher*]."

Some people may question this approach, thinking, *I don't seem to be getting wealthy*. For them, we suggest Rabbi Akiva's second approach in *Bava Basra* 10:

The wicked Turnus Rufus asked Rabbi Akiva: "If your God loves poor people [as is evident from the obligation to give charity], why doesn't He support them [directly]?"

He replied: "So that we should be saved from Gehinnom! When we give charity, we gain merits that provide us with eternal rewards."

Rabbi Akiva himself served as a *gabbai* (money collector) for charity to the poor.

Three Reactions

The Talmud (*Avodah Zarah* 20a) relates that when Rabbi Akiva met the wife of the wicked Turnus Rufus, he reacted in three ways: he spat, laughed, and wept! Why?

1) He spat in reaction to the fact that her physical body originated from a putrid drop.

(This reaction is also recorded in *Avos D'Rabbi Nassan* 16:2, regarding Rabbi Akiva: "He came to a certain country... The ruler sent him two women to entice him... They tried all night to tempt him, but he sat there [retching and] spitting... When they complained about his reaction...he said: 'What can I do? Their odor is to me as disgusting as dead carcasses...' ")

2) He laughed because in a prophetic vision he knew that she would eventually convert and he would marry her.

3) He wept in mournful anticipation of her beauty rotting in the ground.

Thus we learn that laughing is one of many reactions that a Jew must train himself to use.

Sandwiched in between his spitting in disgust to avoid temptation from her beauty and his crying in sadness over the eventual decay of her beauty, which was created by Hashem for a short period in this temporary world, he laughed with joy over her brief opportunity for greatness when she would convert and marry a *tzaddik*.

Rabbi Akiva's trained reflexes for instantly thinking of the humble origin of man's body and its eventual decay were also surely helpful for achieving his unique personal humility.

- The Gemara (*Ta'anis* 25b) says of him that he was extremely humble and yielding in his behavior.

- When he was once insulted by the remark "You have not attained the status of even a cowherd," he humbly replied, "Not even the status of a *shepherd*" (*Yevamos* 16a).

All the Time

A good heart is always celebrating.

(Mishlei 15:5)

A Torah Jew should be constantly brimming with the joy of Torah Judaism, the enthusiasm of Torah observances, and confidence (*bitachon*) that Hashem is doing everything for a kindly purpose. Complaining or worrying about matters other than Torah and mitzvos is against the ideals of the Torah.

For example, people who criticize the weather ("raining again?") are ruining their own days and minds, and undermining those of their family and friends. Instead, we must think of the benefits of rain and learn from children who think of rain as fun, and thank Hashem for another good day. Hashem decides when to make it rain, and He has good reasons for it.

Likewise, all the seasons should be accepted with joy and appreciation. The sunny summer, wet winter, sprightly spring, and brisk fall are all times that are prepared by Hashem and served with tasteful delights. We have to work on ourselves to reach these levels of feeling.

We have to concentrate specifically on the basic pleasures of life, for they are readily available gifts from Hashem. To be able to breathe, see, walk, talk, eat, and drink are pleasures which we must learn to appreciate and thank Hashem for every day of our lives.

The way one looks at the world is the kind of world he shall have.

(*Sing, You Righteous*, p. 17)

The Need for a Teacher

This approach may seem difficult to those who are not accustomed to it. But we must learn, from Rabbi Akiva and other Torah Sages, the way to act and even think.

Laughter is a natural physical and emotional reaction which Hashem has endowed humans with, but we have to learn how to condition our systems to use it properly. Finding things to laugh about daily may be difficult at first, but learning this art is worth the effort.

We also need contemporary *rabbanim* to help us start, to guide us, and to promote this attitude. "Make for yourself a teacher" (*Avos* 1) is a teaching that applies to all aspects of Torah.

Avos D'Rabbi Nassan 6:2 explains that Rabbi Akiva exemplified the *mishnah* "Drink the words of the Sages with thirst" (*Avos* 1). This was evident from his initial intellectual motivation to begin studying Torah and from his approach to actual study.

How did he begin?

He came across a boulder that was hollowed out by a flowing spring. He was amazed. How had this become hollow?

He realized it was by means of the water, which constantly dripped onto it. This caused him to draw a lesson for himself: If soft water is able to penetrate hard rock, surely the Torah, which is tough as iron, can penetrate my heart and body, which are composed of flesh and blood!

He immediately went to study Torah.

Rabbi Akiva interprets a verse of Koheles (7:8) as follows: "The conclusion of a matter will be good if it begins properly from the start." This interpretation follows Rabbi Akiva's insight here, in that as the water initially began to drip onto the stone it immediately began making headway, although it would not be discernable for a long time. This encouraged Rabbi Akiva to persevere in his studies at first even while he was unable to recognize any lasting gains (*Letters of Rabbi Yisrael Salanter*, nos. 10 and 30).

How did he study?

When he began studying the *alef-beis*, he learned first from a rebbe. Then he sat down by himself to question every detail: Why is the *alef* written this way? Why the *beis* this way? He kept at it until he had studied the entire Written Torah.

Then he went to Rabbi Eliezer and Rabbi Yehoshua for the study of Mishnah. After learning each halachah, he would sit by himself and consider: Why is this so? He then returned with his questions.

Positive Thoughts

- Partly sunny weather is the same as partly cloudy.
- One who is forty years old is also forty years young.

- Someone who is colorblind actually has the ability to see several colors. (The Talmud refers to blind people as those with perceptive vision.)

These are some minor examples in which we tend to emphasize the negative unnecessarily.

The *Chovos HaLevavos* (6:6) relates how a Sage heard people complaining about the terrible odor of a dead carcass. His comment: "See how white the teeth are!"

Rabbi Akiva teaches us to always be positive and look for the redeeming factor in all people, things, and situations.

His Teacher

Rabbi Akiva had a great teacher for this subject: "He served Nachum Ish Gam Zu for twenty-two years!" (*Chagigah* 12a). Nachum Ish Gam Zu was famous for his saying, "This, too, is for the good" (*gam zu l'tovah*).

Rabbi Chaim Shmuelevitz, *zt"l*, points out that this Tanna is referred to only by his quality, whereas the title *rav* is omitted. This indicates that this title is an even greater title than "*rav*." We may also suggest that his name, Nachum, which means comfort, is also connected to his great trait. He was always calm, confident, and comforting due to his principle, "This, too, is for the good."

When he was delivering a box of jewels as a gift to the king to gain favor for the Jewish nation, it was emptied (stolen) and refilled with earth. When he discovered the seeming misfortune, he said, "This, too, is for the good!" (*Ta'anis* 21a). Subsequently, a miracle happened rendering the outcome very good.

Now this example raises a problem. If a miracle would not have happened, he would have been in trouble. Was he then relying on a miracle? Is that the logic of *"gam zu l'tovah"*?

This brings us to the subject of *bitachon* (trust in God): "Everything is in the hands of Heaven" (*Berachos* 33b) and "all that the Merciful One does is for good" (ibid. 60b). The more one understands and believes these truths, the more they will work for him. "Blessed is the person who trusts in Hashem, for Hashem will fulfill his trust" (Yirmeyahu 17:7).

Developing *bitachon* does not mean inducing oneself to trust without logic. Rather, it is the awareness that Hashem alone controls everything. The more one realizes this truth, the more he will merit Hashem's obvious control. Hashem decides whether to use concealed methods or obvious ones, and the decision is based on the person's worthiness and level of *bitachon*. Thus Hashem could have helped him in a million ways, but Hashem chose a miraculous method due to his unique greatness.

Seeming Misfortune

A person is obligated to bless [thank] Hashem for misfortune.

(*Berachos* 54a)

The great *tzaddik* Nachum Ish Gam Zu was at one point blind in both his eyes. His arms and legs had been amputated, and the rest of his body was full of boils.

When his disciples inquired how such a perfect *tzaddik* could end up in such a sad state, he replied that he had brought it upon himself by his own request for a punishment for a slight misdeed.

They said: "Woe to us that we see you as such."

He said: "Woe to me if you would not see me as such [if I did not merit the opportunity to atone for my misdeed] (*Ta'anis* 21a).

The Secret

This episode is chilling. How do we understand it? Let us turn the pages of the Talmud for a moment to a similar story with an interpretation by Rabbi Akiva.

> *When Rabbi Eliezer was ill, his disciples came to visit. He said: "Hashem is displeased with me [I am very ill]."*
>
> *They began to weep. Rabbi Akiva began to laugh.*
>
> *They questioned him: "Why are you laughing?"*
>
> *He replied: "Why are you weeping?"*
>
> *They said: "The sefer Torah is suffering. How can we not weep?"*
>
> *He said: "That is why I laugh! When our rebbe was successful in everything he did, I was concerned lest he, chas v'shalom, receive his reward in this world, but now that I see the rebbe suffering, I know his reward in the World to Come is intact."*
>
> *The rebbe said: "Have I failed in any part of the Torah?"*
>
> *He answered: "You have taught us, 'There is no person who is so righteous as to always do good and never sin'"* (Koheles 7).
>
> (Sanhedrin 101a)

Thus we see that Rabbi Akiva's complete faith in the World to Come enabled him to be so bold and react so strongly even when it seemed callous.

For great people, sympathy was expressed by insuring one of his share in the World to Come.

He who laughs, lasts!

Beloved Treatment

The very next piece of Gemara continues with a similar incident:

Four sages came to visit Rabbi Eliezer.

Rabbi Tarfon said, "You are better for the Jewish nation than rain."

Rabbi Yehoshua said, "You are more beneficial to us than the sunshine."

Rabbi Elazar ben Azaryah said, "You are more beneficial than our parents."

Rabbi Akiva said, "How beloved is suffering!"
(Rashi: Because it atones for the person.)

Rabbi Akiva was not merely reacting to his rebbe's plight. He was offering comfort and encouragement to his rebbe. As the Gemara continues to elaborate, a person should study the benefits of suffering and appreciate the goodness that Hashem is sending his way.

Note: It may be unwise and halachically improper for the average person to use this approach when visiting an ill person. However, it may be worthwhile at times to relate this episode of Rabbi Akiva in a gentle, thought-provoking manner.

Variety

What about other forms of suffering, such as mistreatment in the courts or by the government?

The Gemara deals with this issue in *Avodah Zarah* 16b:

> *Rabbi Eliezer was once arrested on false charges. When he was released, his disciples came to his home to console him, but they were ineffective. Rabbi Akiva then asked for permission to repeat a lesson he had received from his rebbe [Rabbi Eliezer]. When he received permission, he spoke:*
>
> *"Perhaps you have derived pleasure from conferring with a heretic, and that is why you were arrested?" [In other words, maybe you deserved it. Thus the temporary suffering that you put up with*

was a beneficial means of atonement for your slight misdeed!]

Rabbi Eliezer responded: "Yes. You remind me of such an incident..."

A Pause for Reflection

Before we go on, let us pause for a moment to study some of Rabbi Akiva's references.

The Gemara (*Sanhedrin* 65a) quotes a teaching of Rabbi Yochanan. (Rabbi Yochanan was a great Sage in his own right. *Tosafos* in *Berachos* 21b says that we follow his view even when he is opposed by Rav or Shmuel!)

- An anonymous *mishnah* is from Rabbi Meir.

- An anonymous *Tosefta* is from Rabbi Nechemiah.

- An anonymous *Sifra* (*Toras Kohanim*) is from Rabbi Yehudah.

- An anonymous *Sifri* (on BeMidbar and Devarim) is from Rabbi Shimon.

All of these are based on the teachings of Rabbi Akiva!

(Rashi in *Bechoros* 30a concludes that most of the *mishnayos* in *Shas* are based on the teachings of Rabbi Akiva.)

> *Rabbi Tarfon declared: "Akiva! Whoever forsakes you is forsaking life!"*
>
> (*Kiddushin* 66b)

> *Ben Azai said: "Alas for me that I did not merit to study by Rabbi Akiva."*
>
> (*Nedarim* 74b)

Bringing Out the Best

Why did Rabbi Akiva merit to have so many great disciples who produced so much Torah?

Perhaps it was his unique skill in bringing out the *best* in others, based on his ability to always see and recognize their qualities.

Dealing with People

There is actually no limit to how far the teaching of Rabbi Akiva extends. "All that the Merciful One does [and did] is for good" includes everything we see, the universe, and all that is contained therein. This brings us to another specific teaching of Rabbi Akiva in *Pirkei Avos* (3:18), which deals with the creation of man:

"He used to say [on a regular basis]: 'Man is beloved, for he was created in the image of God!

" 'How beloved are the Jews, for they are called "Children of Hashem!"

" 'How beloved are the Jews, for they were given the most desirable utensil [Torah] with which Hashem created the world...' "

These are three fundamental lessons in understanding the greatness of man, Jews, and the Torah. They also guide us in dealing with and reacting toward these three.

Rabbi Akiva is especially famous for his teaching that to "love your fellow man as yourself" (VaYikra 19) is the *great rule* of the Torah.

What does Rabbi Akiva mean with this emphasis?

When a potential convert came to Hillel with a request that he be taught the whole Torah while he stood on one foot, Hillel taught him: " 'What is hateful to you do not do unto others.' This is the whole Torah. The rest is commentary, which you must learn."

Now we suggest a further step — to consider this great rule as part of the even greater rule: "All that Hashem does is for good."

Every Jew was created by God, in the image of God, and as part of the nation that are considered the children of Hashem. We must relate to these positive greatnesses in every person we deal with. And we must love every Jew as an extension of ourselves.

Rabbi Akiva taught: "All Jews are children of kings."

Caution

With all his respect and love for every individual, as discussed above, Rabbi Akiva was still cautious with suspicious characters. The Talmud relates (*Avodah Zarah* 25b): Robbers met them on the road, but the disciples of Rabbi Akiva outsmarted them. So they said: "Fortunate is Rabbi Akiva and his disciples, for they have never been harmed by unsavory people (on account of their wisdom in protecting themselves)."

The Supreme Goodness of Torah

The sublime concept of love that was demonstrated by Hashem when He gave us His Torah is a privilege that we have to consider and study all our lives. The infinite greatness of the Torah, coupled with the fact that it was Hashem's tool of Creation, charges us with the responsibility to preserve the entire universe by means of our wholehearted devotion to Torah study.

True, "all that God made is good"; yet the greatest of all goods is the Torah!

(The same verse which Rabbi Akiva uses in *Avos* 3:6 to show that the Torah is God's greatest gift to us is also used in *Avos* 6:3 to show that there is nothing as *good* as the Torah.)

Rabbi Akiva offers a parable (*Berachos* 61b) to appreciate this uniqueness: A Jew is like a fish in water. Other human beings breathe air, but Jews must breathe and exist in the medium of Torah. We cannot exist if we depart from the atmosphere of Torah!

Rabbi Akiva was such an expert at interpreting even the crowns on the letters in the *sefer Torah* (which are halachically required on certain letters to signify the honor due the Torah) that Moshe Rabbeinu exclaimed to Hashem: "Since you have such a person in Your future plans, why bother giving the Torah through me?" (*Menachos* 29b).

This also explains the *mishnah*:

When Rabbi Akiva died, the sublime glory of the Torah came to an end.

(*Sotah* 49b)

A Human Sefer Torah

This teaching will help us understand another unique Torah lesson:

> *Shimon of Amsune had a system for interpreting every "es" [with]in the Torah to include another subject besides the one named in the verse. However, when he arrived at "with Hashem, your God, you must fear," he decided that his approach was erroneous, and he retracted all of his previous interpretations based on his system...until Rabbi Akiva came along and taught that the "es" comes to include talmidei chachamim. (One has to fear Torah scholars as one fears Hashem [see Avos 4:12].)*
>
> (*Bechoros* 6b)

Rabbi Akiva maintained that an authentic Torah Sage becomes as holy as the Torah that permeates his being. He becomes sacred with the Torah that is inscribed in his mind and every fiber of his being to the extent that the Divine Presence of Hashem rests on him (*Berachos* 8a).

Looking Back

As we study these amazing lessons from this greatest of teachers, we anticipate finding the source of his greatness in his background.

Yet upon examining his past we are even more amazed. This giant of Torah Sages had been an ignorant man up till the age of forty, to the degree that he even hated Torah scholars. He had said, "I could bite a *talmid chacham* as a donkey would, causing his bones to break" (*Pesachim* 49b).

Tosafos (*Kesubos* 49b) explains that although he had been a *shomer mitzvos* (mitzvah-observant) and an exceptionally decent person, he erroneously considered Torah scholars to be haughty, and he thought they despised the ignorant.

(We can suggest that his amazing turnabout was triggered in part by his envy of the Sages. At first, he was anguished by his envy, but it turned into motivation to increase his wisdom, resulting in his becoming one of the greatest Sages.)

Looking Further Back

Looking back even further, we discover that his father, Yosef, was a convert to Judaism (Rambam's

Preface to *Mishneh Torah*). This disqualified him from being chosen as *nasi* (*Berachos* 27b), but it did not dampen his enthusiasm and ambition to become the greatest Torah scholar he was capable of being. He excelled to a degree that he was greeted with the following exclamation:

"Are you Akiva ben Yosef, whose name has traveled from one end of the world to the other?" (*Yevamos* 16a).

(The *Mitzpeh Eisan* in *Yevamos* points out that Rabbi Akiva is mentioned in *Shas* a total of 564 times, which corresponds to the numerical equivalent of this praise of him, and the halachah follows his view 375 times.)

A "Good" Helpmate

There is one *tov* (good) that was the catalyst which produced this remarkable dynamo. His chances for success in Torah seemed extremely remote. Until forty years of age, he was a mere shepherd for a wealthy cattle owner.

But Hashem has His ways. Of all the good things that Hashem did and does constantly, there is a unique benefit that is singled out in the Torah for specific emphasis. (We can be sure that this benefit had an exalted pedestal amongst the thousands of lessons that are included in Rabbi Akiva's great teaching: "All that the Merciful One does is for good.")

In the *Chumash* we learn:

> *And Hashem said: "It is not good for man to be alone. I shall make for him a helpmate..."*
>
> (Bereishis 2:18)

Hashem sent Rabbi Akiva a woman by the name of Rachel who discerned the rare potential of this unpolished gem, and she challenged him by consenting to marry him if he would agree to devote himself to Torah study for twelve years. She ignited the spark that triggered his greatness to explode as a raging forest fire to achieve a sensational degree of Torah perfection that illuminated the world for all time.

Subsequently, when her dream came true, Rabbi Akiva declared for all time: "My Torah and your Torah (that of his 24,000 disciples at the time) are *hers!*"

Most of the Torah which we possess today came to us through Rabbi Akiva's disciples. They all benefited from the heroic idealism of this one woman who risked her future to motivate Rabbi Akiva to study Torah.

Rabbi Akiva said: "Who is considered wealthy? One who has a wife whose deeds are beautiful!"

(*Shabbos* 25b)

Good All Around

As we study the ways of this great *tzaddik*, we have to keep in mind the words of the *Derech Etz HaChaim*, by Rabbi Moshe Chaim Luzzato:

Studying the lives of our ancestors provides the road for us to achieve greatness. Consider for a while every day what the great Sages did that caused them to be chosen by Hashem. Then consider how you can emulate them.

Do we relate to the good all around us? Do we accept the reality that Hashem arranged the mate we were blessed with for our benefit?

Self-Esteem

While we are discussing the all-around good that one should discern in other people and everything else that Hashem created, let us not overlook ourselves.

Rabbi Akiva also teaches: Your life precedes that of your fellow man.

(*Bava Metzia* 62a)

Hashem also created *you*! Don't negate yourself and your abilities. Hashem does only good things, and thus, you must be a creation with a tremendous amount of potential good just waiting to be developed.

Hashem does not produce inferior products!

Never Give Up

Let us not think that it was easy for Rabbi Akiva to achieve what he accomplished in life. Besides being a late starter (forty years old), Rabbi Akiva suffered major setbacks in life. He lost 24,000 disciples in one period when they all died during an epidemic. Yet he did not give up. He continued by rebuilding his yeshivah in Bnei Brak with a handful of disciples and succeeded in teaching and nurturing the Sages who subsequently transmitted the Torah to the Jewish nation for all time (*Yevamos* 62b).

Rabbi Akiva's Torah attitude was to do his best with seemingly superhuman efforts and then to continue to do his best when he was pushed down. The concept that Hashem is always doing His best for us, so to speak, should motivate us to always do our best for His sake.

In addition, the fact that Hashem gives a person more time to live is the best proof that Hashem is saying to that person, "Keep at it. The best is yet to come!"

Striving for Excellence

Even after he had attained tremendous greatness, Rabbi Akiva kept striving for even more superior levels. At one point, he even undertook studying *PaRDeS* (the orchard of Secret Studies) together with three other great Sages (*Chagigah* 14b).

Before they entered, Rabbi Akiva issued a warning (ibid.) concerning the hazards of the journey. And of the group, Rabbi Akiva was the only one who entered in peace and came out in peace. He even received protection from Hashem *Yisbarach*, Who proclaimed to the angels, "Leave go of this elderly Sage, for he deserves to make use of My honor!"

It says he "entered in peace," which means that he was fully prepared for this endeavor. He was prepared in all aspects of Torah understanding and character training, which is why he was capable of profiting from the remarkable experience (*Exalted People*, p. 112).

Counting Your Blessings

During a difficult period when they were first married, Rabbi Akiva and his wife were sent a unique message of comfort (which they understood as a message from Hashem). In their extreme poverty, they were living in a barn and sleeping on straw. Eliyahu the Prophet appeared in human guise, begging them for some straw for his wife, who had just given birth, to lay on.

Rabbi Akiva pointed this out to his wife: "Do you see? There are people who have less than we do!"

She responded: "Go to the *beis midrash* to learn [i.e., I'll manage without you]" (*Nedarim* 50a).

Key to happiness: There are always people worse off than you!

Six Doses of Wealth

In his lifetime, Rabbi Akiva became fabulously wealthy six times through Heaven-sent methods [corresponding to the six orders of the Mishnah that he mastered] (*Nedarim* 50a).

This also demonstrates Rabbi Akiva's persistence and determination. He kept pushing forward and facing all the difficult barriers that confronted him. As he succeeded more and more, he was assisted by Heaven again and again in unexpected ways.

Hashem always deals with us in positive, beneficial ways, but the amount of success is dependent on how worthy we are and how much effort we invest to achieve the will of Hashem.

Good Fortune

There is a sensational climax to the close of Rabbi Akiva's life on this world.

First he was imprisoned on the fifth day of Tishrei (*Shulchan Aruch, Orach Chaim* 580:2) by the Romans for teaching Torah in public to gatherings of his disciples.

For this, Papus, who had previously questioned his approach, now exclaimed: "How *fortunate* you are to be imprisoned on account of Torah study; woe to me, for I was imprisoned for idle matters" (*Berachos* 61b).

(Perhaps we can interpret the timely passing of Rabbi Akiva during the Ten Days of Teshuvah as a demonstration that he was the perfect *ba'al teshuvah*.)

A Final Discourse

When they began to execute Rabbi Akiva, it was time to say Shema. They began to tear his flesh with metal combs, while he began to prepare to accept upon himself (joyfully — *Talmud Yerushalmi*) the yoke of Heaven with love.

His disciples said to him: "Our teacher, to this degree?" (i.e., Is it still required for you to say the Shema?).

He replied: "All my life I have been distressed because of my desire to fulfill the verse 'Love Hashem, Your God, with...all your soul [life].' " This was explained by Rabbi Akiva to mean, even when He is taking your life (*Berachos* 61b). He kept thinking: *When will the opportunity come my way so that I can fulfill this great demonstration of my love of Hashem. So now that the opportunity did come my way, shall I not fulfill it?*

The Key

From Rabbi Akiva's last words we gain an insight into his approach to greatness. He had been striving all his days to achieve all he possibly could. Every mitzvah that came his way, every Torah goal that he could dream of, he worked on persistently with constant determination. Even that which he could not do himself he wished for and prepared himself to fulfill to perfection, if and when the opportunity came his way.

The Underlying Message

He extended his saying of the word "echad" [Hashem is One], and his soul expired while he was thus engaged. A Heavenly Voice proclaimed: "How fortunate you are, Rabbi Akiva, that your soul left you while you were saying 'echad'!"

(*Berachos* 61b)

What is the connection between Rabbi Akiva's life theme and the word *"echad"*?

"Hashem" denotes God's mercy (*Rosh HaShanah* 17b and *Tosafos*). "Hashem is One" refers to the unique Oneness of Hashem Who rules the entire universe and controls and conducts all nature and all of history with His system of perfect mercy and kindliness.

Thus, Rabbi Akiva, who lived his life based on the principle, "All that the Merciful One does is for good," was actually proclaiming this teaching of *"Hashem echad."* This was the final close of his great lesson plan for life in this world.

"Hashem is One" implies:

- There is no other force that operates independent of Hashem. Thus all happiness and seeming misfortune come from Him alone.

- He is One and the same in all that He does: "Hashem is just in all His ways and kindly in all His deeds" (Tehillim 145:17), without exception.

- He is One forever. He endures forever, and He is the same forever. He is One in this world, and He is One in the Afterlife (Rav A. Miller in *Praise My Soul*, p. 309).

Heavenly Fireworks

The Gemara (*Berachos* 61b) continues:

The angels said to the Holy One, blessed be He: "Master of the Universe, is that the reward for Torah?" (Is it fair that this great Torah Sage should suffer in this way?)

Hashem replied: "Their portion [that of the righteous] is in [eternal] life!"

And then a Heavenly Voice proclaimed: "Fortunate are you, Rabbi Akiva, for you are *prepared* for immediate entry to the World to Come!"

You have perfected yourself by living with the proper preparations. You knew all along that everything in life is good and that the Ultimate good is yet to come. You prepared yourself with Torah and mitzvos and the proper Torah attitude, and now you will receive the greatest of all good for all eternity!

Steps to Success

This section consists of a variety of mind-openers to help motivate us to follow in the footsteps of Rabbi Akiva. Having departed this world when he was 120 years old, this great Sage is compared to Moshe Rabbeinu, Hillel, and Rabban Yochanan ben Zakkai, who also lived their full lifespan of 120 (*Tosafos, Bechoros* 58a). When he started his career he was unknown, ignorant, and forty years old.

What did he do right?

Many things. For us to really get it right we must study all of his teachings and the entire *Shas*. For a start in that direction we offer these selections and a final reminder:

Train yourself to always say: "All that the Merciful One does is for good."